How a Book Is Made

written and illustrated by

Aliki

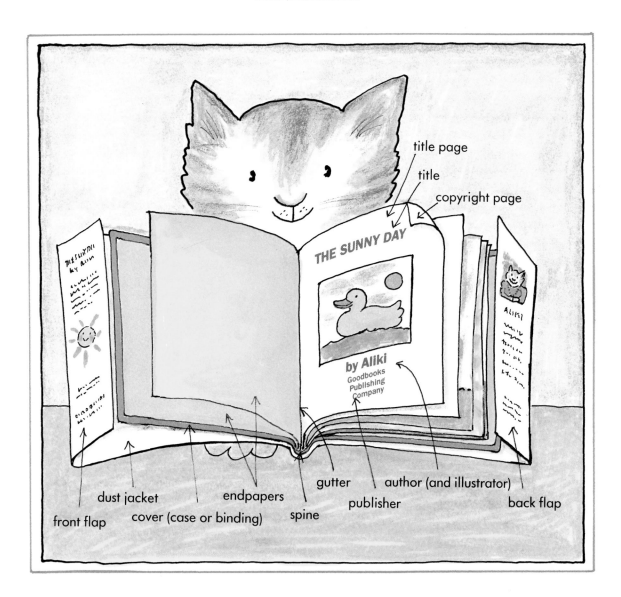

title page

title

copyright page

THE SUNNY DAY

by Aliki
Goodbooks
Publishing
Company

ALIKI

gutter

author (and illustrator)

dust jacket

endpapers

publisher

back flap

front flap

cover (case or binding)

spine

HarperTrophy

A Division of HarperCollins*Publishers*

to Margaret Clark

The various steps in the making of a book can differ from one publishing house to another;
this book shows how *this* book was made.
For their valuable and generous help, I am grateful to all
whose jobs are mentioned in the book, especially John Vitale,
Carolyn Otto, Lynnet Wilson, Sue Curnow, and Zig Ruskin.
Thanks most of all to Ginny Koeth, Al Cetta,
and

Barbara Fenton
Editor *extraordinaire*

How a Book Is Made
Copyright © 1986 by Aliki Brandenberg
Printed in the U.S.A. All rights reserved.
Designed by Al Cetta

Library of Congress Cataloging-in-Publication Data
Aliki.
   How a book is made.

   Summary: Describes the stages in making a book,
starting with the writing of a manuscript and the
drawing of the pictures, and explaining all the
technical processes leading to printed and bound copies.
   1. Books—Juvenile literature. 2. Book industries
and trade—Juvenile literature. 3. Publishers and
publishing—Juvenile literature. 4. Printing—Juvenile
literature. [1. Books. 2. Book industries and trade.
3. Publishers and publishing. 4. Printing] I. Title.
Z116.A2A42 1986   686   85-48156
ISBN 0-690-04496-8
ISBN 0-690-04498-4 (lib. bdg.)

   (A Harper Trophy book)
ISBN 0-06-446085-1 (pbk.)

First HarperTrophy edition, 1988
Published in hardcover by HarperCollins Publishers

I like books.

I like the way a book feels.

I like the way a book smells.

I like to turn each page,

read each word,

look at the pictures.

Who made this book?

Author-Artist (Illustrator)	Editor	Publisher	Designer	Copyeditor-Proofreader
Production Director	Color Separator	Printer	Publicity and Promotion Director	Salesperson

"I did," says the author-artist.

"We did," say the editor, the publisher,

the printer, and many others.

They all did.

Many people made this book.

And this is how they did it.

A book starts with an idea.

The AUTHOR thinks of a story.

She writes it down.

It is harder than she expected.

Sometimes she can't find the right words.

She has to look things up.

At last she is satisfied.

She sends off her MANUSCRIPT

to her EDITOR at Goodbooks Publishing Company.

The editor likes the story. The PUBLISHER likes it, too.

The editor sends the author a CONTRACT.

A contract is a promise. The publishing company will manufacture, publish, and sell the book, and pay the author a ROYALTY. That means the author gets some money for each copy of the book sold. The more copies that are sold, the more the author earns.

The ARTIST also gets a contract.

In this case the author is the artist.

She will illustrate her own book, so there is only one contract.

The author-artist signs the contract.

The author's work is done for now.

And now the artist's work begins.

9

She chooses the size and plans out the pages.

Then she makes a handmade book called a DUMMY.

She designs the dummy the way she wants the book to look.

The artist shows the dummy to her editor.

The editor makes some changes in the TEXT.

The DESIGNER makes some suggestions for the art.

They choose a TYPEFACE for the text.

The COPYEDITOR checks the spelling, grammar, and punctuation.

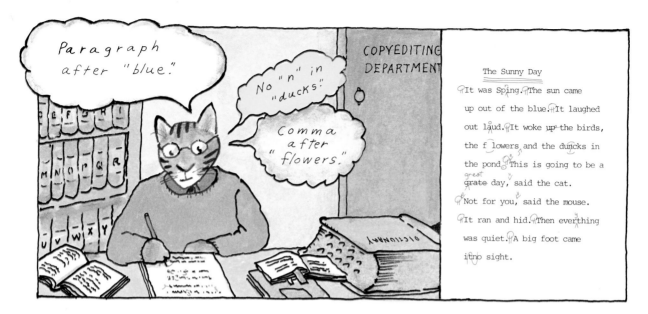

The designer sends the edited text to the typesetter,
where it will be SET into TYPE on GALLEYS.

12

floppy disk

typestyle disk
with all the letters
of the alphabet
in one typeface

The text is typed into a computer where it is stored in code on a magnetic tape or floppy disk.

The floppy disk is put into a TYPESETTING MACHINE, together with a typestyle disk. Letter by letter, the coded text is transferred from the floppy disk and set on PHOTOSENSITIVE PAPER in the chosen typeface.

The paper is developed, and comes out with the text printed on it in one long galley, which is then cut.

The PROOFREADER checks the galleys.

Another set is sent to the author-artist.

Now the artist has more to do.

She prepares the FINISHED ARTWORK.

She uses the dummy as a guide.

Each page is drawn separately and measured exactly.

one spread (two pages)

gutter (where the book will be sewn)

trim lines (where the pages will be cut)

Page 4   Page 5

The art is in FULL COLOR.

It looks the way it will in the printed book.

It is a long, hard job.

The finished art is delivered.

The artist's job is done.

The art is checked for any mistakes.

Then the PRODUCTION DIRECTOR makes COST ESTIMATES and a PRODUCTION SCHEDULE and orders PAPER for the books.

The designer makes MECHANICALS.

They show exactly how the text and art will fit together.

He pastes the galley type onto OVERLAYS.

The art and mechanicals are sent to the COLOR SEPARATOR where FILMS will be made.

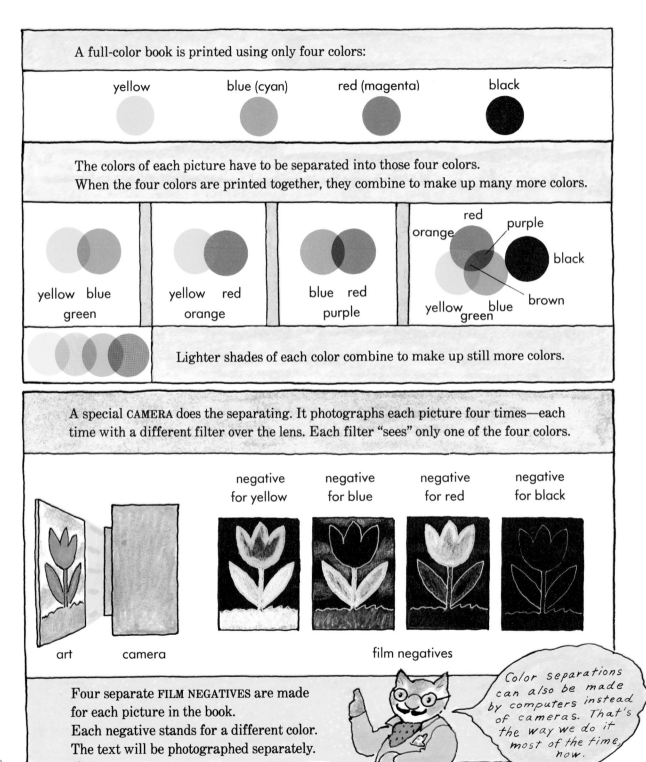

A full-color book is printed using only four colors:

yellow   blue (cyan)   red (magenta)   black

The colors of each picture have to be separated into those four colors.
When the four colors are printed together, they combine to make up many more colors.

yellow blue
green

yellow red
orange

blue red
purple

red
orange   purple
black
yellow blue
green   brown

Lighter shades of each color combine to make up still more colors.

A special CAMERA does the separating. It photographs each picture four times—each time with a different filter over the lens. Each filter "sees" only one of the four colors.

negative for yellow   negative for blue   negative for red   negative for black

art   camera   film negatives

Four separate FILM NEGATIVES are made for each picture in the book.
Each negative stands for a different color.
The text will be photographed separately.

Color separations can also be made by computers instead of cameras. That's the way we do it most of the time, now.

18

Sometimes the art is PRESEPARATED by the artist. A separate overlay is made for each color. The overlays will be photographed to make the film negatives.

← overlay

← register marks to keep the separate overlays correctly lined up with one another

The art is painted in shades of black. The shades of black stand for shades of the four different printing colors. The artist has to know all the color combinations and how to show them in shades of black.

The films are put together by the STRIPPER.

The films for the separate pages are stripped together on big plastic sheets to make FLATS. Each flat has films for one color on it. A "window" is cut in the plastic behind each film.

Then PRINTING PLATES are made from the films.

There are separate plates for each color.

— frame

— film

— plate

Each flat is put into a frame together with a thin metal PHOTOSENSITIVE PLATE. The film and the plate are pressed together and exposed to strong light. The light shines through light areas of the film onto the plate. It cannot shine through dark areas. And it cannot shine through the plastic around the films, either.

— plate

The image from the film now appears on the plate. (The exposed areas, where the light could shine through, will hold the ink and print the color on the paper.)

19

The plates are used to make COLOR PROOFS.
The proofs will be checked to see if the printed colors match the artwork.

color proofs (progressives)

The four colors are printed separately, then in combinations, and then all together.

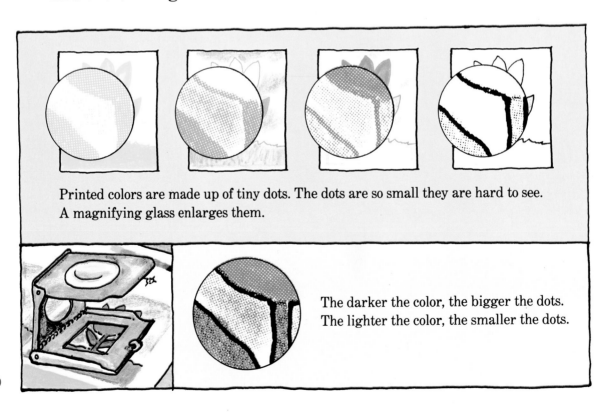

Printed colors are made up of tiny dots. The dots are so small they are hard to see. A magnifying glass enlarges them.

The darker the color, the bigger the dots. The lighter the color, the smaller the dots.

The color separator looks to see if the colors are too strong or too light. Through the magnifying glass, he can see if the colors are properly REGISTERED— that the dots are printed in the right positions.

Everyone checks the proofs very carefully.

Corrections are made on the films and new plates are made.

A final proof is printed and approved.

The films of the art and text are put together and exposed to light to make a BLUEPRINT.

This is the last chance to check and correct the films.

Now the set of FINAL PRINTING PLATES can be made.

All thirty-two PAGES are arranged so that they will print on one big SHEET.

Some pages are upside down.

After the printing, the sheets will be folded again and again.

Each page will fall into the right place.

Sixteen pages are on one side of the sheet...					sixteen pages are on the other.			
1	91	ƐI	�'t		Ɛ	'tI	SI	ᄃ
8	9	12	5		6	II	10	7
∠I	ᄃƐ	bᄃ	oᄃ		bI	oƐ	IƐ	8I
24	25	28	21		22	27	26	23

The COVER and JACKET will be printed separately

FINALLY...

The plates are put on the big cylinders
of a FOUR-COLOR PRINTING PRESS.

The book goes "on press."

After months of preparation, the printing takes only a day.

The noisy four-color press is in a huge room with other presses.

Inside the Four-Color Offset Printing Press

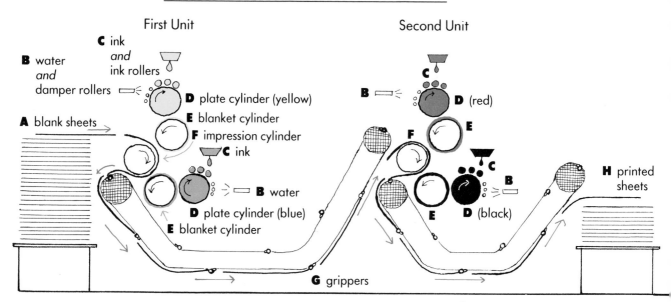

First Unit

Second Unit

C ink *and* ink rollers

B water *and* damper rollers

D plate cylinder (yellow)

E blanket cylinder

F impression cylinder

C ink

B water

D plate cylinder (blue)

E blanket cylinder

A blank sheets

B

C

D (red)

E

F

C

B

E

D (black)

H printed sheets

G grippers

Enough sheets are printed to make all the copies of the book—
first one side of the sheet, then the other.

The first sheets are checked. When the color is perfect, the rest of the sheets are printed.
When one job is finished, the machines are cleaned for the next job.

Each unit of the press prints two colors at a time.
The inks and the machinery are controlled from the CONTROL PANEL.

1. Blank sheets **A** are stacked at one end of the press.
2. The plates on the plate cylinders **D** are dampened with water **B** and inked **C**.
3. The image from each plate is printed onto the rubber blanket cylinders **E**.
4. As the sheet passes between the first blanket cylinder **E** and the metal impression cylinder **F**,
   and then between the impression cylinder and the second blanket cylinder **E**,
   the ink impressions from the blanket cylinders are printed onto the sheet.
5. Grippers **G** pull the partially printed sheet to the next printing unit.
6. After four color impressions, the printed sheets **H** are pulled by another set of grippers
   and stacked at the other end of the press.

The press can print thousands of sheets an hour.

The PRINTED SHEETS are sent to the BINDERY.

Sheets are cut in half and then folded...

into two SIGNATURES—sixteen pages each.

They are FOLDED,   GATHERED,

The signatures are still folded at the edges.

The edges are trimmed off.

SEWN,   and TRIMMED.

One sheet has become thirty-two pages.

A hard COVER is made.

A machine makes a hard cover, called a CASE or BINDING.

cardboard glued on cloth or paper

edges turned up and glued down

This casing-in machine puts the cover on the book.

Gluing the ENDPAPERS to the cover holds the pages in the book.

dust jacket

THE SUNNY DAY
by Aliki

cover

A DUST JACKET is wrapped around the book.

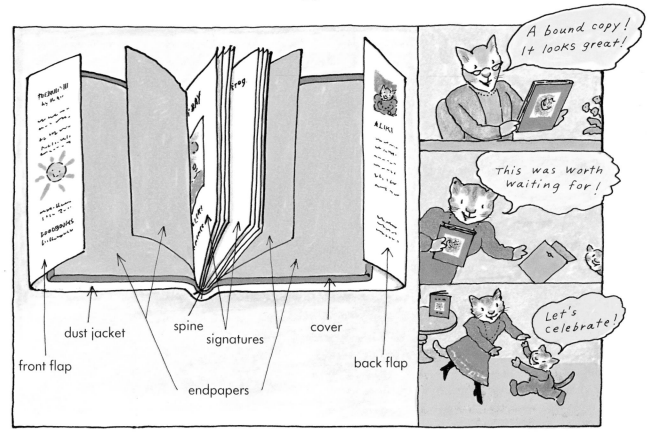

dust jacket

spine

signatures

cover

front flap

back flap

endpapers

A bound copy! It looks great!

This was worth waiting for!

Let's celebrate!

At last—a BOUND BOOK!

The bound books are taken to the warehouse and stored.

The editor presents the book at SALES CONFERENCE.

Copies of the book are sent to newspapers and magazines
and to librarians.

The book is talked about and REVIEWED.

Librarians buy copies for their libraries.

The SALESPEOPLE sell the book to bookstores.

One day Father sees the book. He buys it.

A book for me!

I can read it.

I can smell it.

I can keep it forever.